To Jenny
with love
Merry Christmas
1985
Mommy

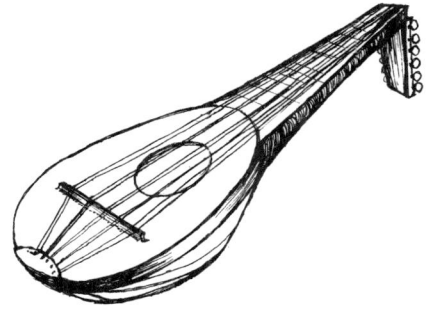

the Song of francis

by fray angelico chavez
illustrations by judy graese
the northland press
flagstaff, arizona

Copyright © 1973 By Fray Angelico Chavez
and Judy Graese (Illustrator)
All Rights Reserved
Second Printing — January 1974

ISBN 0-87358-105-9
Library of Congress Catalog Card Number 73-75205
Printed in the United States of America

the song of francis

 WEEK of centuries ago, in the little city of Assisi in Italy, there lived a boy whom everybody knew as Francis. There still were knights in those days, and often Francis saw them riding through the cobble streets. Sometimes it was a single knight in quest of adventure; or there was a whole company of them on their way to war.

On big festive days they held jousts or mock battles in the main square, while jolly minstrels, or troubadours, went around singing songs about famous knights. They told how Roland had died fighting the Saracens, and how Galahad and the other Knights of the Round Table had sought the Holy Grail.

Francis and his playmates watched the knights closely, to learn their saddle poise and their skill with the sword and lance. They also listened carefully to the minstrels, to learn by heart those wonderful gay ballads of knighthood. And though Francis was somewhat smaller than his companions, he was equal to the best at playing knights. And none had learned the troubadour songs as well as he, nor to play the minstrel lute. Besides, he had a clear sweet voice which even grown-ups loved to hear.

Master Peter Bernardone, who was Francis' father, was greatly pleased with his son. As the boy grew older, he bought him a real sword and a fine horse; later he got him a suit of armor with all the silken clothes and tinted plumes that went with it. For Master Peter was quite a rich man. He was a merchant who brought precious silks and other costly cloth from foreign lands to sell to the wealthy princes of his own country. When Francis became a famous knight, Master Peter told himself, the rich family of Bernardone would become a noble one besides.

But Lady Pica, Francis' gentle mother, thought otherwise. She had given Francis a lute because she loved to hear him sing, and also because she herself was from the Provence in Southern France, the land of the minstrels. But her chief reason was that a mother prefers a lute to a sword. However, she remained quiet when Master Peter talked about Francis and horses and battles. Only when other ladies told her that Francis would surely become a famous knight someday, would she answer them, saying:

"Someday my boy will be a son of God."

It was whispered about that Francis had been born in a stable, like the Christ Child. At that time, they said, Master Peter was away in the Provence buying goods. When the hour arrived for Francis to be born, it did not happen. Neither the physician nor the ladies helping knew what to do. Then a strange old woman came into the room and said that the baby would be born readily if the mother were carried out to the stable. And so it came to pass.

Maybe this was true, and that is why Lady Pica spoke that way. And maybe Francis also knew about it, somehow. For when he sang the songs about Galahad and the Holy Grail, there was a soft faraway look in his eyes. Even when he was telling his father about his dreams of knightly adventure, and of serving great kings someday, his gaze seemed to go past the princes and castles of this world. Master Peter did not notice this, but Lady Pica did.

His playmates also caught him with this look in his eyes. They teased him often, calling him a dreamer. But there was no meanness in their teasing, for they were very fond of Francis. He still could fight as well as any of them, while he sang and played better than they. Yet he never boasted about either. And to those who were not quite as rich as he, he gave many things that their own parents could not afford.

As these lads of Assisi grew into young men, they used to gallop through the town in full armor, to hold tournaments in the square or out in the open fields. And always at their head rode Francis. At night they went from inn to inn, drinking toasts to their future triumphs and amusing themselves with the merry tavern girls. Francis himself would play the lute and sing, and everyone listened, for his voice had grown richly mellower, and he now composed songs of his own about brave knights and fair ladies.

To match his voice, there was something about his lean dark face and slim body that drew the eyes of others to him, even strangers. Watching his soft dark eyes as he sang, or his slender fingers on the lute-strings, both men and women beamed happily, and their hearts went out to him. His companions, of course, were very proud of his gifts. And the girls who served wine in the taverns paused to look and listen.

But even though he laughed with them and teased them at the tables, these girls could never bring themselves to put their arms around him, or sit on his lap and kiss him, as they did with his friends. Some lasses said that Francis made them feel as though they were his very own sisters; and one does not flirt with one's own brother. Others declared that his eyes seemed to look straight through them.

"It is as if Francis sees something bright and beautiful that we ourselves cannot see," all of them said.

"Aye, he dreams that he is Sir Galahad and has just seen the Holy Grail," his companions laughed. "Or he beholds some fair lady waving her scarf to him from her tower window."

Francis would only smile. Yes, he did see something very beautiful that one might find in pretty maidens and shining gold cups and glistening silver armor. But if you would have asked him what it was, he would have spread out his arms and shrugged his shoulders. He did not know himself. It was as though his own desire had leaped from his breast and was flying ahead, like a bit of the sun or a bird of fire, beckoning him to follow. Sometimes he managed to catch a glimpse of it, like a splinter of light that vanishes around the corner of one's eye.

Because Francis was happy by nature, he greatly enjoyed jousting and riding with his friends by day, or singing and drinking with them at night.

Yet he felt strangely sad when his dream or desire came, only to flee ahead of him like a vanishing bird. Was it because knighthood was still so many years away? He had begun to notice how his father, although he always made more and more money, was not perfectly happy. Neither was his good mother, although she had all the things a wealthy lady could own. His companions and the giggling girls had a lot of fun, too, and still their joy was not perfect.

Perfect joy. This is what he eagerly yearned for. He wanted it not only for himself, but for every man and woman and child. A true knight, thought he, wayfaring with stout arm and heart from land to land, had the best chance of finding that joy in his wide wanderings. By vanquishing base men and fierce beasts he would clear the countryside of every evil and set the people free from sorrow and fear.

And someday, like a pot of gold at the end of the rainbow, he would come upon perfect joy. Meanwhile, he kept his mind's eye searching for that bright something which, like a burning bird, kept hiding from sight behind every hill, every tree.

FRANCIS and his mates had already passed their eighteenth birthday when their big chance came at last. There was a large city that wanted to bring little Assisi and neighboring towns under its power. When the nobles of Assisi called for volunteers to help defend their countryside, Francis and his company put on their armor and rode forth singing to meet the foe. They were excitedly happy, for they were sure that some great prince would see what brave warriors they were, and then invite them to be his squires. And before long, after more victories and deeds of derring-do, they would all be dubbed knights at last.

But the would-be knights were woefully disappointed. Instead of shining like heroes, they were all captured early in battle. Then they were thrown into a castle prison, where they lay all but forgotten for almost a year. With nothing to do in that dark and lonely dungeon, the companions of Francis and the other prisoners used to grumble all day and all night, when not quarrelling among themselves. But Francis sang the old songs of knighthood as well as ballads and ditties that he was always making up. His eyes sparkled when he sang, as though they caught a glint of light other than the faint sunbeam from the high-barred window. This made the others very angry at first. They told him that he had gone crazy for sure.

Francis would only laugh and say: "Why should I not be merry, for someday I shall be a great knight, and the whole world will admire me."

This sounded so outlandish, and yet Francis said it with such gentle earnestness, that even those prisoners who had not known him before almost believed him. They still laughed at him, but somehow they felt better for the time being.

At last the young prisoners were set free and allowed to go home. But, sad to say, the many months in a dungeon had done much harm to Francis' spare frame. For weeks Lady Pica had to tend her grown son through chills and fevers, as she had done when he was a baby. But all the while she was praying over him and smoothing his brow, his feverish mind and heart kept searching for that something he could not describe. He was sure to find it, he kept telling himself, when he grew strong enough to ride away in full armor once more.

Weeks later, when he found himself well enough to stroll out of the city, the fleeting brightness of his quest did not show itself among the trees. The once merry meadows seemed so bleak now, and the once charming woods looked so dreary. He wondered if he had let his thinking drift too long in boyhood dreams. No longer a lad, he must put away the things of a child, and from now on seek his life's goal as a man. This thought refreshed his mind, and soon he began feeling well and strong again.

Master Peter Bernardone, who had become sad and moody while Francis was ill, grew happy and noisy once more. Both father and son started talking in earnest about knighthood and making plans. At this very time, minstrels from the Provence came singing about a most valiant knight, Sir Walter by name, who was doing great deeds for God and country against powerful invaders from the north. Here, said Master Peter, was the best chance anyone could have to become a famous knight.

Francis needed no coaxing. He would join Sir Walter and learn all he needed from the best knightly teacher in the world. And filled with renewed hope, his father bought him the best suit of armor that could be found anywhere.

But Francis did a strange thing on the day before his departure. On the outskirts of Assisi he met a real knight who had lost everything in battle, even his armor. Without even pausing to think, Francis gave him his own. Of course, he did not tell anyone, much less his father, but went and polished up his old armor for the journey.

And that very night he had a dream, a dream so clear and beautiful that it seemed real. He found himself in a gorgeous palace hall within a castle. Its walls were hung with knightly shields covered with shining crosses. And seated on a throne was the most beautiful bride one could imagine. Then a voice told Francis that all this would be his someday. The damsel would be his bride, and the shields would belong to his own soldiers.

Right away, and even after he awoke, Francis was filled with the old joyful daydreams of boyhood, something he thought he had put away for good. That afternoon, at a farewell party which his friends gave for him at one of the inns, he told his old companions and the serving girls that now he knew for sure that he would be a great prince someday.

   The very first night of his journey, Francis had another dream, or rather, he heard the same voice of the other night's dream calling him by name. He could not tell whether he was asleep or awake, it sounded so real and clear when it asked:

   "Francis, is it better to serve the master or the servant?"

   "The master, of course," Francis answered.

   "Then, why do you go forth to serve the servant?"

   Francis could not reply. Coming to himself and sitting up, he thought that he caught a glimpse of a birdlike flash in the darkness. Again, it was his old boyhood desire, like a bird playing hide-and-seek, but impossible to find. And yet, the voice that still echoed in his ears seemed more real than the flash.

   Now wide awake, Francis asked aloud, as though

speaking to himself: "Lord, what will You have me do?"

And now the voice sounded more real than ever. "Francis, return home at once, for the dream that you had could have different meanings, you know."

FRANCIS rode back home, so much troubled in his mind that both Master Peter and Lady Pica thought the dungeon sickness had returned. This is why Master Peter did not scold him for failing to join Sir Walter's army. Besides Francis began to show some interest in the family's import trade. While it pleased his father, it helped Francis think out his long, long thoughts. And his mother was so happy that her son had not gone to war.

Of evenings Francis wandered off to the taverns to meet his old friends, to treat them and sing the old songs for them. But his voice was no longer the same merry voice. His eyes still seemed to dream, but there was little or no sparkle in them. Because he barely nibbled at the bread and cheeses on the table, and scarcely touched his wine cup, his friends and the inn girls teased him gently, saying that poor Francis must surely be deeply in love.

Smiling back, as always, Francis answered with a very serious tone: "Yes, I am thinking of marrying the noblest and prettiest maiden the world has ever seen."

For their teasing brought back again that dream which had seemed so real, the bride on her throne and the castle walls hung with shields. For a moment a light came into his eyes, and he felt as though he had almost caught sight of the bird of perfect joy.

Remembering how he had almost seen it when he gave his armor to the poor knight, Francis

began giving his entire allowance to the beggars
of the city; some of his extra clothing went to poor
families he knew. At these times he felt closer
to that beam of joy, which had to be from Heaven,
surely, as had been that twice-heard voice.
As it became more and more clear to him that
he was not meant to be a knight in armor, was it a
sign that he must be some sort of knight in rags?

There was a pilgrimage passing through Assisi on
its way to Rome. Francis joined it, hoping to find an
answer at the tomb of St. Peter. There he found
more beggars than he had ever seen gathered in one
place, and from all parts of the world. Trading one
of his changes of clothing for a beggar's rags, he
began begging at the church door every day,
later giving the coins he collected to the neediest
among the paupers.

But while he did enjoy playing the role of
a beggar, and then helping others thereby, he soon
realized that the joy he sought was not to be

found in simply begging for alms. Only once did he catch a tiny glimpse of the bird of joy, flitting among the pillars of the great church, but it might have been only the play of sunlight from the windows high above as a pigeon took flight.

More bewildered than ever, Francis returned to Assisi. As his father was away doing some buying, he turned to the beggars again, inviting them to receive food at his father's table and pantry. Lady Pica helped him, but all this had to stop when Master Peter was expected back. Still, there was no answer to his puzzle. Francis began thinking that his misery would never end -- until one bright and beautiful morning when he followed an urge to mount his horse and take a ride out in the open country.

Warm and clear was that day, with red poppies and white daisies splotching the green roadside, like a precious French tapestry which his father had brought Lady Pica last year. The larks and thrushes called to each other from the woods and meadows, like lutes that no man could

ever hope to make and play. The towers of
Assisi, and of neighboring castles on the hilltops
all around, fretted the round horizon like a
fairyland. His horse pranced gently as if enjoying
the smell of every leaf of grass and the caressing
comb of sunlight on his white coat.

Not since he was a dreamy lad had Francis realized
that the earth was indeed a beautiful place to live in.

Suddenly, the tinkle of a bell jerked Francis from
his reverie. Not far ahead off the road stood a leper,
calling for alms with a voice like a rusty hinge.
A murky shadow fell upon the world, it seemed to
Francis, although there were no clouds overhead.
His stomach began churning a sickening taste
to his mouth. Quickly he spurred his horse so that
he could gallop past with held breath until he
was well out of sight.

For to him there was no more hideous sight than
that of a leper. In those days, anybody who had
festering sores that would not heal was considered a

leper. There were no medicines or drugs in those times that might have easily cured them. And so they were chased from towns and cities to live alone in the woods and fields where their sores spread all over their poor bodies. To warn people of their nearness they were made to carry a small bell and beg from afar.

But Francis of a sudden pulled hard on the reins with one hand as he reached for his coin pouch with the other. If it was good to help ordinary beggars in town, how much better was it to help these sorry wretches who were suffering not only from want and their painful sores, but most of all from loneliness and lack of love. Instead of tossing the man some money and riding speedily away, as folks usually did, he found himself dismounting right next to the leper, as if his steed had been told to draw up next to him.

And as Francis slowly placed the coins in his hand, and he looked into the unhappy eyes in that swollen, stinky, purple face crusted over with matter and blood, he let go of the reins, hugged the leper with both arms, and then kissed him on either cheek.

    And then the world around lit up with the golden glow of that winged sun or burning bird which he had lost long since. As he often used to say afterwards, he was filled with utter sweetness of soul and body. He had not yet seen the bird of perfect joy, but here for the first time its splendor had surrounded him like a golden tent.

FROM that day on, Francis helped the wandering lepers and dressed their sores. In a little house in the woods where there were those who could no longer walk and beg, he spent hours comforting them. And still, though he knew that he was doing something highly pleasing to God, he no longer felt that golden brightness around him. It had lasted only that first day.

As at other times, once in a while there was a faint flickering along the fringes of the leafy woods surrounding the leper hut. It always seemed to disappear towards an old but pretty wayside chapel in a pleasant valley nearby, the little church of San Damiano.

One day, saddened more by his bewilderment than anything else, Francis knelt in prayer inside San Damiano. If only the Lord would tell him exactly what to do. Where was that beautiful palace of his dream? What meant those knightly shields along the walls, if he was not to be a knight in armor? And who was that bride whose beauty he had not yet seen among the fairest ladies of Assisi and neighboring towns? If he had both felt and seen the splendor of perfect joy when he first kissed the leper, where had it gone? And why?

Praying thus in his heart, Francis heard a voice calling him. He looked around the seamed stones and cracked plaster of the ancient walls, and then up to the weathered rafters where some sparrows had ceased their chattering and were cocking their downy heads to one side. Again the voice called his name. It was the voice of the castle dream, and it came from the plain altar table where a ray of light had fallen on the large crucifix upon it.

This crucifix was much different from those we usually see now. It was made of wide flat boards put together. Two panels were stuck on either side under the arms. Instead of being carved in the round, the crucified figure was *painted* on the cross's flat surface. Much smaller figures of saints were outlined in bright colors on the side panels, and still smaller angels covered all other spaces. The rest of the cross was bordered with lines and scallops in red and black and yellow.

It was a very fetching cross, if rather darkened by age and because the church had so few windows. However, more than a ray of stray sunlight was lighting it up now, as if that long-sought bird of joy hovered behind it. In fact, to Francis' eyes this cross did have the shape of a bird, as of an eagle flying. And the halo shimmering along its edges was like that fleeting glow which had escaped him so often, ever since he first noticed it as a dreamy boy.

Now he heard the Crucifix of San Damiano say plainly in that same wonderful voice he now recognized: "Francis, repair my church which, as you can see, is falling down."

"Gladly will I repair it, Lord," Francis cried out.

At once his heart and mind and the entire church were filled with that same joyful light which had enveloped him when he kissed the leper. Its glow flowed from the halo of the cross, as had the voice itself. Then, they were the same, the voice and the light! Here, at last, dwelt the bird of perfect joy!

Even after the light faded away, and the sparrows above began chirping once more, Francis knelt as in a trance. How good it was to be here, he kept saying again and again. From now on this would be his dwelling, too.

But the Crucifix did not speak again, nor did the glow along its edges return, no matter how often Francis came back to kneel and pray before it. For a time he sighed aloud and squinted his eyes while wishing hard with all his heart, but the sparrows kept on cheeping while the place seemed gloomier and the silence deeper amid their chatter.

Then he saw how foolish this all was. It was not he who had caused those fleeting glimpses of the bird of joy ever since he could remember. When he hugged the leper, the light that drenched his soul and all the world about him had come of its own accord, and when least expected. So also had it done when the cross spoke to him and the sparrows ceased their chirping. They knew better.

Meanwhile an echo within his ear kept on saying: "Build my church, build my church..."

FRANCIS went home for what money he had, to start repairing the roof and walls of San Damiano. Since this was far from enough, he foolishly took bolts of fine cloth from his father's storerooms and packed them on one of the horses. Then he took them to a big city market to sell. Francis did not think he was stealing, for he considered this a part of his inheritance.

He not only sold all the silks and satins and brocades, but the horse as well. Then he returned with a purse full of gold for the priest of San Damiano. But knowing Master Peter's temper only too well, the priest refused the money. Still, he let Francis lodge with him in his poor hut by the church. Francis then tossed the purse on a high windowsill, and he himself began hauling stone to repair the building. Most passersby who saw him were now sure that the son of rich Peter Bernardone had gone completely mad.

When Master Peter returned to Assisi and found various things missing, there was more than the devil to pay. Not only had Francis squandered away his precious stuffs and a fine horse, but he was disgracing the family by acting like an insane beggar. This was the worst blow. Fuming with rage, he went after Francis, ready to tear him apart.

At first, Francis was so scared that he hid cowering in a cave for many days. But soon realizing that this was the wrong conduct for a knight of the

Lord, he trudged back to Assisi to face his father. The fickle townspeople, who had once loved him so much for being a happy-go-lucky lad, now crowded down upon him, pelting him with sticks and stones and calling him names. After kicking and cuffing him in front of everybody, Master Peter dragged his son home and locked him in a vault of his storerooms. It had an iron door and looked exactly like a jail.

Poor Lady Pica tried to keep Francis as comfortable as she could in this home-prison. Then, one day when her husband went away on a long business trip, she turned him loose and sent him away with her love and blessing. On his return, Master Peter was angrier than ever, since he had hoped that Francis would have come to his senses by this time. Now he asked the sheriff to arrest Francis and have him tried for theft.

On seeing the constables coming toward him with chains and fetters, Francis ran into the bishop's palace and asked for refuge. Since the hue and cry raised was about money that he had already given to the church, he thought, only the bishop's court could try him. For at this time he had retrieved the purse from the high windowsill at San Damiano in order to present it to the bishop. And so the sheriff's men turned away to report this new twist to Master Peter.

Bishop Guido of Assisi, who had a most understanding heart, gave Francis shelter and promised to judge the case. And in no time Master Peter with a mob of curious citizens pushed into the bishop's parlor snarling for his money. The bishop listened patiently, and then said to the angry father: "Master Bernardone, by every right the money belongs to you."

Turning to Francis, he continued: "My son, you did a noble thing, except that the horse and goods did not *yet* belong to you. What is more, God does not want money which a stingy owner does not care to give. Return the purse to your father."

Stepping forward before everyone present,

Francis handed over the money pouch. Then quickly pulling off his cloak and shirt, then his shoes and his long breech hosiery—even his undershirt—he cast them all at his father's feet.

There he stood for the moment naked before the wealth and power of the world, feeling as free as his horse when the saddle and other harnessings were removed after a hard ride. Or like a dove or a hare when released, after long imprisonment, from its cage. No one moved or made a sound as Francis spoke calmly but firmly:

"Until now I have called Peter Bernardone my father. But because I mean to serve the Lord alone from now on, I return not only his money which troubled him so much, but also the last stitch of clothing that he gave me. From now on my only father will be our Father Who is in Heaven."

Bishop Guido stood up and covered Francis with one end of the purple mantle that he wore, while Master Peter and the spectators backed away and out of the palace. Later, at the bishop's request, a servant brought a peasant's shabby grey gown, and the bishop put it on Francis with a prayer. And then Francis went happily away with the kindest of blessings upon his head.

For Bishop Guido had been deeply stirred by all that he had seen and heard, and he knew that the light in the young man's eyes was not the wild gleam of madness but the promise of something wonderfully good.

As he went out joyfully into the open world, Francis felt like the day he kissed the leper and when the Crucifix of San Damiano spoke to him. Again he caught glimpses of the bird of perfect joy leading him on as it vanished behind the town houses, behind the hills and trees of the countryside. But now he understood that he could not catch up with it on this earth. The vision of it was to be seen only in Heaven. Yet he also knew that its light would always bathe his heart from this moment on, not merely at certain times, because now he belonged to God completely. And nothing in this world would belong to him.

This was perfect joy, to serve the Lord daily as His knight, without a home or a sword or a horse or anything. His princely palace was the whole beautiful earth, roofed over with the blue sky and carpeted with the grasses and flowers. That most beautiful bride of his dream—he had found her at the moment he returned his last piece of clothing to Master Peter in order to enter her bridal chamber.

It was Lady Poverty whom he had seen before, but never recognized, in the beggar and the leper, in the poor little church of San Damiano. Yes, this was his wedding day, to the sweetest bride in all the world whom he would never let go and whom the world could never take away.

FOR years and years Francis went about from town to town, from city to city, through woods and valleys, calling on people to love God and one another. For God was so good, and so were all the things that He had made. In the beginning, folks took him for a madman because he was so happy even when they mistreated him. In those times there were other men who went around preaching poverty and penance; they had long sour faces and blue noses and melancholy eyes. At the same time they foretold the end of the world and cursed both princes and priests who loved the things of this world too much. And so they were considered holy men because they could not even smile.

But because he laughed and sang, Francis was thought to be crazy. Because he neither cursed nor criticized others, but blessed everyone instead, prince and pauper alike, he must be out of his mind.

Little by little, however, the light of his inner joy began to catch, and soon it spread like a grass-fire throughout the land and far beyond into surrounding countries. Calling himself the knight and herald of the Great King of Love, he showed people how religion could not be the sad thing that others made it. And all the earth, and everything on it, were altogether good because God had made them all.

By and by, others joined Francis to learn the secret of his joy, although they never became quite like him. The first companions were a rich merchant, a learned lawyer, and a farmer; then a knight and a priest. They gave up all they had to give it to the poor, and put on the armor of Francis, which was his grey peasant gown tied around with a knotted rope.

These were his Knights of the Lord's Round

Table, he often used to say, never forgetting his dream. With the years more and more men of every class became part of his happy band, all pledged to serve Lady Poverty, his bride, she who had lived close to Jesus from the day He was born in a stable to the day He died naked upon the cross.

Many, many books, big ones and small ones, have been written about Francis and all that he did and said. It would take a big library to hold them. They tell in words and pictures how Francis loved the wild birds and animals of the forest, and how they surrounded him to hear him praise the Maker of them all, the songbirds finally joining their voices to his.

They tell of beautiful songs he composed about the Lord as his troubadour, but also about this good earth which God had made for men and all living things, calling all of them, whether great or small, his very brothers and sisters. His

Canticle of Brother Sun and all the Creatures has regaled the minds and hearts of people ever since; in it he praises the Lord through Brother Sun and Sister Moon, through Brother Wind and Sister Water and all created things.

Those many books also tell how a noble damsel, the good Lady Clare, left her castle to serve Lady Poverty, and how Francis placed her and her sister and other gentle ladies in San Damiano, there to be the nightingales of God in the dwelling place of perfect joy.

They tell how through joyous tenderness he tamed not only the heartless robbers of the woods and highways, but even a big, bad wolf which was ravaging the farms and villages; and, harder still, how he prevailed on folks to lay away their weapons and live in peace like true brothers and sisters.

They tell how he made the very first Christmas Crib to delight children of every age for centuries thereafter; and how new warmth and goodness came into the churches and homes when princes and priests, merchants and monks, poor folks and rich folks, learned that true joy is not to be found in hate or envy, in pomp or in pride.

They tell how he went alone to the Holy Land in order to convert the Sultan, a Saracen monarch whom everybody feared; yet that supposedly cruel man was so taken by Francis' simple joy that he treated him with every kindness and let him return home unharmed.

These and hundreds of other things they tell. But, most wonderful of all, they tell how Francis did see at last, even on this earth, *the bird of perfect joy.*

SOME twenty years had flown by since the day Francis had heard the Crucifix of San Damiano and then had taken Lady Poverty for his bride. They had been so many years of perfect joy, in spite of the pains and disappointments to be found in this world. Filled with this joy of serving his Master so closely, all that Francis wished now was to die and see the source of perfect joy face to face.

One quiet day Francis was praying, as he often did in late months, on the top of a very pretty mountain, called La Verna. It reached up to heaven like praying hands. The tips of the fingers were great rocks or crags at the very crest. Among these, under great green trees abloom with singing birds, Francis was praying that day when a sudden blazing light filled the mountaintop.

Brother Falcon, a hawk that stayed with him day and night, froze perfectly still. And all the birds in the trees, even the very leaves, hushed up together as Francis looked up and saw floating above him what seemed like a great bird of throbbing fire. It made him think right away of the Crucifix of San Damiano, except for the blinding splendor of it.

Yet his wide-open eyes could look straight at it, just as if one were able to stare straight into the sun without being blinded. It was like a bird, indeed, for it flew like one, like a great hummingbird hovering before a lily or a rose. But instead of two wings, it had six. The two largest wings were folded downward in the shape of an eagle's body; two others flitted on either side like ordinary wings; two smaller ones curled upward as if to form a halo about the head. And all of them had quivering golden flames for feathers.

It was like the description of certain angels, called *seraphim* that Francis had read about in Holy Writ. These fiery beings hovered about God, loving him with perfect joy and burning zeal forever and ever. This is how Francis had always wanted to love and praise God.

But this was no mere angel. In the midst of those fiery wings Francis made out the crucified One of San Damiano, bright as the enfolding wings, but with the gentlest look imaginable on His glorious face. And the wounds in His hands and feet and side sparkled like stars.

How long the vision lasted, Francis could not tell. He felt he had melted from that joyous heat and light. For at last he had seen what he had sought for so long, the *bird of perfect joy*.

When the light had faded away at last, Francis found himself looking at his own hands and feet. They hurt like burns, and on them were wounds like those of the vision. They were bleeding around what seemed like black riveted nails formed from his own seared flesh. And then he felt on the left side of his breast a larger wound, like the one which the lance made in Jesus' heart.

Francis thought for sure that he was going to die then and there. But, no, he lived on for two more years, years of mingled joy and pain that drank up his strength. One pretty autumn evening, which he knew to be his last upon this earth, he called together those of his companions who were staying with him. They took up his little body, which had shrunk to the size of that dreamy boy of long ago, and they carried him from the crisp dusky air into a little mud hut. This was his castle where Lady Poverty reigned; along the walls hung little willow crosses, the swords and shields of his knights.

In spite of his great weakness, Francis began to sing with that clear voice of his boyhood, not the minstrel songs of Roland or Galahad, but his own Canticle of Brother Sun and all the Creatures. At the end he added a new verse—about Sister Death who would soon take him by the hand and lead him to perfect joy itself.

Finally, Francis asked to be laid on the bare earthen floor, undressed as on the day he wed his Lady Poverty in the bishop's palace, and he spread out his wounded hands and feet like the Crucifix of San Damiano. And so the dreamer of Assisi fell into his last sleep with a smile on his thin dark face.

And then the little larks, which never fly at night and never go into houses, came in from the darkening fields fluttering and twittering in circles over the still form of their little brother, their blessed brother, who even in this life had found and seen the *bird of perfect joy.*

Printed at Northland Press, Flagstaff, Arizona
Typography and Design by John Anderson